Bleeding Hearts

a poetry collection by,
Nicholas Thomas Durham

NICHOLAS THOMAS DURHAM

ISBN: 0692285199
ISBN 13: 9780692285190

Dedication

This is dedicated to all of my friends and family
who all taught and showed me how to live a rich life.
This is for you guys Mom, Dad, Celeste, Danielle, Alex,
my extended family I love you all. Also to my good friends
Tyler Rivord, Craig Hatch, Eric Burns, everyone else you
know who you are,
and also to Matt Dillard and RJ who first pushed me to
write.
Thank you all.

Acknowledgements

Eric Jonathon Pino for your photography and art for our cover.
Tyler Rivord and the Rivord family for presenting avenues for
my work's publication.

Table of Contents:

A Day's First Light

Bestow on me your every beauty,
your very touch,
your very grace.

Become for me a shining light
a glowing beacon against the coming night.
Against the tide of restless shadows,
combatant to the ever growing black.

Break forth from the endless void with all of your radiance.
With all of your burning aura,
every bit as bright as the fiery sun.

Become for me a guardian angel.
A glimpse of heaven within a world grown dark,
and fight off the demons that lurk within the shades.
Obsidian pools where once festered,
the nightmares begin to bubble and rage.

Give to me yourself in all of your purity,
and let me bask in an age of tranquility.
Give to me all it is I desire.
A peace found wound in revelry
and a heart,
braised and set to fire.

Grant me this very wish,
to hold and capture you all for bliss.
And embark towards a new world to start,
as within you I will find my saving Ark.

In these for breath I must fight.
Gentle curves down a milky back,
pursed lips curled in all of their playful pout.
Oh how your flesh consumes me,
as now it has become the only thing I see.

Be to me the only gift I seek,
and be not afraid to stay with me until the brink.
For love, endearment, redemption, and the golden shore,
all of this and more.
I have already set aside for you,
so long before.

A Look Into the Horizon

Comparing you to splendors held in perfect worlds
the sincerity of their settling snow is but a chill,
unmatched and unfavored to your features,
and how the waves of dark hair rests upon it so.

    The rebirthing sun
illuminating dormant life is only mere sight,
unless if gazed upon by your eyes reflection.
Only then, does these eyes awaken.

    A dove's calling
although haunts,
is nothing to your voice's whisper.
Could the coming tide followed by thunderous skies be as endearing.
With that I doubt.

For only the sinking sun
casting amber clouds
one with the untamed blue
can be compared to you.
In why I must wonder how to feel such beauty
for which only my eyes can reach,
just before I sleep.

A Realization of What You Are.

I can hear people whisper under their breath about it,
    just like a whole new folk's tale coming to life.

It's something in everyone's mind
    but something that nobody can find.
No matter how hard we try.

But I swear to you that one day I thought that I had caught a glimpse of it.
    In between the leaves lying next to the murky water I saw it.
I can remember the very spot where I laid my head next to that heavenly company.
    And in a sense,
I can still feel it every time I walk upon that unforgiving grass.

But once the double take has passed
      the feeling evaporates back into the air it came from.
And as I try to recollect, and force my eyes to remember
      what exactly was it that I had found.
I begin to wonder,
      could it be something in which I've already known
but never did uncover.

      I cringe as now I can completely realize and now can plainly see.
That what I had found was an undeniable love.
      And what was it that I had seen through the leaves and laid
      next to,
why,
      it was you.

Black Bird

She was just like the raven
standing out in the cascade of blue
so damn beautiful, as if it was all I knew.

The black bird that caught my eye
from the canopy of indigo dye
an image, that presses me into asking why.

Why is it that my arms can't take flight,
just another household pigeon
still stuck in my iron barred prison.

But I'm still struggling towards my ambition
of open skied admittance,
flying laden with a hopeful mission.

Of being one with her and sky
trailing in the current as the clouds go by,
and now I can no longer wonder why.

Why I can't help create the breeze
instead I flutter with ease,
within these talons I hold heaven's keys.

In vain I searched for them in the weight of the world,
and found them once I turned my back to ground so cold
as I levitated past with the hand I hold.

I used to pluck the feathers that I once had lacked
flightless wings now covered in shining black,
my past hopes are now nature's fact.

As I go side by side against the blowing gust
with that black bird that had bound my lust
whose wingspan, now holds all my trust.

There's no need to search for something new
or the rooftops that once we knew,
my home now is within the blue, circling right next to you.

Comets Crashing

Come crash onto me,
as the comet upon the sea.

Come screeching across the sky,
burning impressions within the eye.

Come bury deep within the wave,
quenching the thirst I do crave.

Whisper softly to me my dear,
intentions these ears long to hear.

Wake the heart's internal beast,
and lay yourself down for the feast.

Why is it I should wait,
for longing often breeds forth hate.

So let us intertwine one in one,
let not the empire say they've won.

Sly past their oppressive intentions,
their preconstructed moralist conventions.

Succumb instead to the yearnings of your bed,
the groaning desires combating in your head.

Lay not still here with me,
with impatience I'll upturn the once calm sea.

Listen as the waves crash over my dear,
an ocean of perfection, with no need to fear.

Love shall once again set free,
the tormented hearts of you and me.

Break forth from these chains we hold,
I am tired of lacking a life so bold.

Become that comet, that solitary heaven's drop,
who did cause the gasp, the heart to stop.

Beckon forth this soul's earth and moon,
as beneath your eyes I do confess and swoon.

I shall make of you a sacred monument,
of which I shall lay forth my every lament.

In the evening we will make our most cherished hour,
of each other's passions we will bask and devour.

Impressions bestowed upon heavenly grace,
we shall embrace upon this very place.

There is no better time than this to see,
our every desire towards ecstasy.

Think not on past faults and reason,
for to not love now, will be the heart's greatest treason.

Then take up my every hope and do not go,
I am stating our very salvation so.

Come shake up this soul's foundation,
you forever shall be my greatest temptation.

Come crater into my every part,
and forever imprint yourself upon this heart.

Come create burning visions for the eye,
setting fire to the once dull sky.

Oh come with comets crashing casted forth from heaven's calling.

Ghosts From the Barstool

I should no longer be the one that you hold onto my dear.
For I have strayed far into the winding of the darkened road,
where the sun is always setting
and the bourbon flows just to drown out man's wonder.
Among companions I yell,
More drink!
As we deflower yet another bottle.
Let us toast to the capturing of our wants!
Either riches, or glory, or to the ghosts of the women in our beds.
Which mine has long been haunted by you.

Bewitched daily with the thoughts of you,
and then driven mad
by the glimpses of your shadow following every step I go.
Until the long awaited night
where it all can be forgotten.
When the whole world is blurry
and the hands and face are numb,
Numb to the hurtful shivers brought forth from a memory.

So what is it that you'd have me do love.
Forget all that's passed,
and become as tranquil as the breeze flowing through a mountain's pass.
Be as simple of a man as the slowly stretching emerald grass.
Give up my very want, my every lust.
You were my victory over hatred, my uphill battle, my loss.
Once the entire world had ceased pleading because of you.

But that was then and this is now.
And as if to say I mourn for you
my eyes glisten back,
staring hard from the reflection in the glass.
Penetrating deep into the depths of a man
that had let such a love as yours,
slip so far from the grip of his hand.

Long Lost Within the Maze

If I had one wish,
it would be the life that I had once knew,
and the time that I had spent with you.
The now forgotten skies
that had set so easy within my eyes.
The grey embedded deep with blue
of the most unforgiving hue.
But I can longer try to hide
the daydreams,
and what they provide.
A disregarded life filled with wonder inside,
and without a presence,
burnt with pride.
But as I try to decide
which exit it is I should find,
the casket, or the struggle hidden in mind
that needs a solution to unhitch the bind.
Was it in you that I can discover
the love that I had never found in another,
the kind of shudder

that I could only find in November's slumber.
Or is there another remedy to ponder.
But despite the facts,
it's only in your premonition that I can react.
With a cold sweat and flutter of vision
as if I did see an apparition.
Of the dream that needs payment and admission
if to see or hear of her permission,
to explore the depths in which you've been missing.
Of the vast and wonderful maze
perplexing the path in finding her ways.
But I have memorized every craft and every turn
that has left me out to burn,
Oh, have I lost and learned.
In my ambition to uncover
the kind of man that suits a lover,
an uncanny survivor, or the ruthless marauder.
But at the end of the day, I guess it's safe to say.
That I can never amount to the standard
in which gives light to the lantern.
That paves your calculated ways
towards the distant home and untouched pattern.
That I can never have conceived or had planned around with,
my sense of hope, or count out step lists.
Because your expectation of comfort and securement,
did never amount to me, or my undying endearment.

My Queen, My Love, My Torment

I t is only I my love who you should stand beside. Who against your fears and torment can hide. For it is I, willing to abandon all my pride. Leave it behind on the shadowed road, or cast it down the rocky side. I will ransom my life if you will it be. So say it so, command me your unmoving servant to which ever means seems fit. Condemn me to the gallows, or a hardened life so trying and hollow. Either fate would never feel so sweet if dealt by any other hand. Send me to the far corners of the earth to use me, exploit me, to lose me. But where ever it is I shall go, to the frozen shards through fields of tundra, to the fires of unending Sahara, or to the forever turning corners in the maze of a hungry jungle's horrors. Where ever it is the white sails take me, my only thoughts will be that of you my love. With the dark lashes and soft pink lips of the cruel mistress who has done this to me. Who has forced my hand to wage war and gorge myself sick in its baths of gore, if only, to leave her without wanting more. Oh all of the blood that I would shed for but a single bat of her eye. May this stand not as a testament towards my anger, but instead a scarlet premonition of a lover's ambition. It was her beauty that first drove me to adopt in practice, the way of life with sword and malice. The culmination of all my lust could splinter every wall to dust. Could split the very foundation of this Earth, and within the flame drown and cast away the sea. I will raise the Kraken from its restful death, and with the monster of the haunting depths, shatter every single port and village left standing here for rage to pillage. And even with all of this, I still must strive to see her smile. What need could she ever have in another? And do not dare stir your tongue and say, it is you. It is you who knows nothing of love. But oh I do understand what it is you call love. It is what I have been long without, it is what in my mind have seen, but have never truly felt. It is the absence that has created the void, burying itself beneath and blackening my already vengeful soul. It is for a man like me the sun, the sky, the salvation from earthly pride. It is a fresh breath, a long sigh, the relieving cry. It is a reason, a meaning, and the act of redeeming. It is the beauty that I have felt from you. Don't you see it is I who can only love you, for it is I who truly needs you. Not the one who uses and exploits you, but I, the one who will face every blade of this world, let alone a hell of fire if only to appease you. And I will gladly thank the one that tears me apart, if it all amounted to just a single day. With the sun and sky held high, a hopeful bottle of deep dark red wine, and a few precious seconds, of only you and I.

Pleading for Atonement

As I put into perspective all of which I yearn for, all of that which will consume this rabid heart, and turn fair petal from stone. I can imagine in one place. I can see it deeply embedded in the back of my eyes, so that even while I sleep, I must be reminded of her ever ending embrace. She is wearing me down now to the point where I am afraid to drown. I have forever lost my foolish pride to the depths of those lashed deep dark eyes, and it haunts me so, wondering how will I ever cope with her straying so far. To see her no longer even with eyes wide shut. I have collected all of the ransom demanded of me by my wants, but I still have yet to find a single drop in any wishing well. Just like my faith they have all but dried in time. So which superstition must I go pay homage to, which sacred place must I go so that peace I can one day know. And once I get there, how much gold is it I must throw. Must I bow down to the dirt which is ultimately all that I am worth. But without the revival for my mind's survival, I am not yet ready to face my dust. I am not yet ready to just simply walk away from it, the life, the love, and the lust that had once bound my heart in trust. A place which is now completely set a flame, and rages more and more with each passing breath. A storm of fire much different from the same old timid flame that once had lain. A pilot light that burned ever so slight, but whose spark had always shown. A tiny speck of warmth which every time I had ever found myself in roving want. Would guide me back and remind me once again, of that radiant light gleaming against the coming night. That bright shine which trails the love of mine. The blinding glow which has penetrated this already darkened soul, finding a home in what is now my sinking throne. And with the fit of rage felt from losing the great crusade, with your coy indifference all to blame. I will force all of the oppressed beneath me, to pile up the crumbling streets a bonfire to set about our feet. I shall use the maddening hatred of the timid flame to light the way as I claim my reign, the newfound king, the first of my name. And while my memories of her are being sent to the awaiting gallows, we shall spread the flame and destroy these once great halls of marble. So that we can one day rebuild this once grand palace of marvel. But first you must pass me the torch and step back, as we begin to watch the monuments I have built for you. And the churches along with its shrines and holy places of my Rome slowly begin to burn. And only the faint trickle of a tear will form, for those streets in which I used to roam.

Sinfonia del Nostro Cuore

(Our Hearts' Symphony)

Oh sing sweet cherub.
Sing soft,
sing long.
Sing with an allure to grace's coming.
Sing a song of endless summer,
of hearts capture and wonder.
With a honey dipped tongue,
speak your hymn and rhyme to set me asunder.
And once splintered and shattered
set me back together within verses of completion,
in flowing measures of unending redemption,
grant me hope.
Within this glory birthed through composition.
Hope from the discontent of endless trial
somewhere where I can revolve and spiral.
Down past the torment into glowing fields of rapture,
send me far,
my bewitching captor.

Far from the rumble of hateful battle
calling to war my heart in the enthralls of struggle.
How I despise the mockery of truth within the masquerade,
their scripted summary of how it is to end the day.
Instead let us play on just so.
Play on my wayward virtuoso
and dance with me to the beat.
Let us both conjure up the dead
with the music now raging inside your head,
and let our hearts' symphony reverberate without end.
Echoing from York to Rome
a perfect harmony unlike any they have shown,
filling the greying dead of monotone
with the beauty of melody that I now behold.
For it is in you that can spark the world to hear,
not just for today,
but from here unto a thousand years.
Such music that can wash away the world in tears
all from the heavenly notes ringing clear.
Brought to life in the fiery fits of passion
something primal,
something beautiful,
something that alludes all our fear.
From only you my dear.
So sing,
sing for me that seamless vision,
that masterpiece within the awakening.
And conduct yourself deep into the everything
while my soul is still there for the taking.
The curtain has yet to draw and close
bringing a sorrowful end,
to the grace and beauty you now transpose.
Why then cease with this.
A final act to alight their ears,

just one more passage I must hear.
For one last resounding crescendo
echoing the rhythm you now bestow.
Will only leave wanting more,
and oh,
how your voice is opening heaven's door.
So sing so softly,
much like the ever rolling sea
with waves of soothing sound,
come wash away the rough in me.
In a tune as bold as thunder
awake our heart's in inspired hunger.
For forever this shall be our theme,
a song hummed by playful things.
The concerto born between two lovers,
of one who could listen until oblivion
till his head did ring,
and an angel,
who loves to sing.

The Desert's Siren

She is a mirage within the dying desert,
with a beauty resembling the calm cool sea.
Light blue eyes peering through the steppes of sand.
My minds been playing tricks
ever since the last few drops of water.
But with just the sight of her,
in the parched thirst I no longer falter.
I'll stay here within the made up vision,
chasing the dark sinking pools that look all too real.
And even though I'm damned
to forever trudge through desert sand.
I'll soon forget the burning once I can catch a glimpse again.
Of that projected beauty cast from fields so lonely.
Oh how quickly that picture can put this mind at ease.
The phantom awakening of a perfect lust,
hidden deep within the waves of rolling dust.
The thought of what these eyes could see.
The premonition, the apparition,
the desert's sweet sounding siren.
The mirage of her getting further lost,
right along with me.

The Essence of a Daydream

Amongst the cold
of November morning,
I find myself beneath the ever changing leaves
the only thing for certain.
Along with the sound of
walkway's rocks
Crackling, Crackling, beneath my feet,
I can hear the faint trickle
of distant water.
Forever flowing toward the river's end
only to be soaked up,
and convinced
to start all over again.
The flicker
of a pale sun's rising,
catches the eye
from branches above.
As bitter air shows
to the world,
with heaving chest

and shortness of breath.
Thin smoke passing
from these sorrowed lips.

I cannot withstand
the shaking of careless hands.
Its convulsions reminds
of how the brain cannot find,
just how to set
the aching body's peace of mind.
Instead spinning thoughts
leave a bruised and battered being stranded,
stranded and searching,
searching for the saving oasis.
Topaz water to bring some comfort
within the desert so dire.

But once the angelic water
has all but dried,
leaving only
a scorched coarse pile of sand,
where to next.
Into the far distance
never finding
what is sought after.
Beside names forgotten
buried far beneath
the broken rubble,
I think not.

Instead I will drain
into the world about me,
like the rumbling of black clouds
propelling heavenly drops

that slowly caught
and rolled,
tumbling far
from edges of red
and yellow leaves.
And like being torn from the branch
I will
without resentment.
Float on by
with no destination,
forever stumbling
and rolling
down the unmarked road.
Until one day
the wind finally decides to stop.
And for once
this worn out leaf
can quietly come drifting down
to the rock.

These Woods I Wander

The changing seasons have come so fast
since I had last seen you in my troubled past.
A time unfulfilled, brooding, and beset,
plagued with adorned racked contempt.

But I have yet to see such skies of blue,
such distant clouds of gray.
Whose thunder mirrors that of my pride
as it was left to scream and die.

But I have long changed.
My eyes no longer see as bright in the day,
or as dim in the moon's glowing light.
The sound of lazy waters upon the tired rock,
splash and hum to ears that for long
have been muffled to its song.

But the biting autumn wind
now that,
that I shall always feel.
Not because it awakes dormant life,
but because it's cold has rendered my soul.

I am now left to wonder,
as the trees surrounding
are quickly shrugging and casting off,
once treasured leaves without a second's pause.

And as the scent of maple fills the air,
I am only left with traces of soft lavender aroma
that had once flown through tinted hair.

That smell that makes my heart flutter,
and my teeth cringe and shutter.
While I bare ivory fangs towards my unknown captor
just as the wolf does once chased after.

Is it she who is hunting me.
Or is it I who is the untamed beast
tracking the scent towards the kill.

Prowling up and down this darkened wood,
searching for that lonesome prey
that I have followed for far too many days.

But even as I rear upon hind legs to strike,
and so viciously dig teeth into rose colored flesh.

Just know that even a beast so fowl as I
will all but whimper and cry.
If stuck with but a single look
from you,
and your oh so piercing eyes.

Violet Sky

Beneath a violet sky
   swaying as she walked by,
I'd dare not speak.

   Lose yourself in me
if only to find,
   a little peace for sleep.

My skin's flushed red's gone white
   at the sight,
of you with him.

   The one I'd wish to be,
the one that took my seat,
   how I hate the way it seems.

And now I'll tremble in lasting misery
   as it's plain to see,
that there's no you and me.

I'll take up the scoundrel's life
and devout it all to strife
    if only, to make the wrong feel right.

Yet it's such a crying shame
    that in dreams you'll still remain
and me, never to be the same.

    So what is left in me
but to break and sink,
    drowned in your deep blue sea.

I can't seem to find
    a reason or rhyme,
to make those teal eyes see.

    That right here next to me
is where you were born to be,
    just rest your bones and dream.

In me is where you'll find
    a repose to sullen minds
from here, until the rest of time.

    Why then do I have to plead,
searching for some stillness in me,
    oh how this heart does bleed.

To show you a different light,
    to show you the distant side,
where you were always mine.

    Won't you meet me there
beyond all worry and care,
    but only if you dare.

To take the step unknown
　　unto splendor's home,
where glory's light has shown.

　　Radiating while the day is fading,
bringing to life petals in the dark
　　a whole new world to start.

As we both shall play the part,
　　not of star crossed lovers,
but that of souls torn so far apart.

　　Bound to in one another
rediscover the other half pulled asunder,
　　can't you feel the mystery and wonder.

Of the life that always was,
　　a love to give Aphrodite pause,
all of this I'm just saying because.

　　You look so lovely in this light that streaks
highlighting the curves of your cheeks,
　　so won't you just stay and speak.

Of a time with just you and me
　　beneath the violet sky we'll be,
at peace, just like two waves at sea.

Vivant (Long Live)

⌒

I will one day pay for the mistakes of my youth. I will have to come to atonement with all of my failures, with all my fears. Although I am still young and my heart pounds away with the promise of full life, yet the wars that wage in mind have aged me. I have been scarred and withered while they have taken me over piercing mountains high, to the darkest valleys below. I have seen my own mortality. Looked deep throughout the course of life, and oh what sights I have seen. I saw much pain and reveling, I have seen torment and defeat, a heart depraved and raped with mistreat. But I have also seen unending beauty, symphonies of beckoning grace, visions of such a perfect place. I saw peace intertwined within the vines and blooming branches, of a vast and cultivated garden, untrodden on by careless feet beyond my own. Throughout the course of my journey I have learned some precious secrets, and the hard taught facts. I have swallowed the most bitter of pills and inhaled the most sacred of flowers, all of which gives the hue of life behind mine eyes. I have been taught to regret, to wallow and lament, led on by the pains enslaved through rife remorse. I have also been told to repent, to cherish and bask within the sweetness of victory, and finally to fall intoxicated with the bliss of a lover's mystery. Oh the lessons of life these eyes have beheld within torn reflection. I hold these treasures dear to my heart my love. I have begun to live with full force, cast hard my swelling tide upon the beach. I fear with full resolve, and fiercely love with an entire heart. You were the Eve that brought upon my entire faults and opened my eyes to my humanity, and oh the mother of my awakening, the creator of my heaven and my hell. I am whole heartedly grateful that she had a face such as yours, such an impossible beauty that even the gods did envy. I would not succumb towards any realization to a beauty that was less than this. But yet how could I let them win? The Brutus within the ranks came along with brothers, who crept by with the faces of friends, with the laughter of companions. It is they who have pierced my heart, and left me to shutter along with the dayflies damned from the start. What was the fault within me that brought about this fate? I was not ambitious nor vengeful as the emperors of old. I did not lay claim or ask of more. All that I had strove for was to pass the quiet day alongside with the one I hold. If this be my tragic flaw then bring forth the spears, call upon the legions and cut deep, for I drank deep from her cup my friend. Oh yes, that chalice overran from the brim as I lay drunk from her embraces, from a long drawn kiss. And this! This is what brought forth their vengeance? The fact not that I loved them too little, but that I loved her too much. As their own loves lye pitiful with long spats of silence and uncare. Their loves are but an empty shell a shadow of what we were, with half hearted grasps and meager promises of minds inept. My love was young, it was pure, with the full life and fiery passion that spring can barely imagine. A love such as this does not come once a life time, but once an eternity. Oh we are such fools my friend to give it all up in the end. To let supposed loved ones give away our salvations, our second comings. You see, mine was with her a revision of a beautiful life, which was laid to waste never again to be replaced. And was this just another lesson in life, a moment passed by with the time of a second's tick? No, this was earth shattering and redefining, one for the books amongst the burning passions of Venus, contemporary to the ones that doomed Troy. And this too I must learn to forget. I will one day pay for my mistakes, my missed chances with what I would have done, what I should have done, and with what I have yet to do. I will one day forget the hand upon my heart, and continue down this road. I have both loved and lost, learned and remembered, dreamed and lived. And despite the transgressions laid down by these hands. I still search upon the quietly passing horizon, amongst the crowed of never changing faces. I count fast the faults within my dimly forged world and slowly think upon its past beauties, with its once sweltering summer days that had left me in a constant daze. But this to must pass and will someday be transformed as the earth with time, the sheer rock with water. And as for us, we will one day forget her touch dear heart, but not yet, not yet...

Wildfire

Come set the spark for me
I'm lonesome and wary,
your gasoline.
Set fire to this kindled soul
igniting everything I did know
oh,
how I could watch you go.
Burn up in me
the simple fool that you see.
I want to be touched by your fire
the kind that burns with pleasure,
my sick desire.
Licked in flame I'll take the blame
if the world,
we do set on fire.
But burn baby burn,
how the flames keep getting higher.
Spread and scorch in wildfire,
consuming everything in a blaze
ever so dire.

All the while for you,
this pyromaniac will perspire.
Don't you see this is what I need
as in the heat my lust does bleed.
So go ahead and burn on brighter,
melt away poor old me
in a sea of unquenched fire.
Within the raging inferno
make of me rubble and ash,
be the matchstick to my destruction
the carful art of torched seduction.
With the beating of my heart
set the stage for charred affection,
your burning fervor is mere perfection.
If I be the tinder and you the lighter
then I'm going to die by fire.
for I've got a smoking disease,
the firebug reeling in need.
All from the overwhelming addiction
that is our bodies friction.
Forever of you I'll desire
my Electra,
my ember,
my fire.

Wildflower

Oh vengeful friend
oh bitter fool.
Do you not see,
there is no difference between you and me.
No enmity
no strangeness.
Just as you I have learned to love
and taught in the simple art of hate,
yet we wonder why nothing will change.
The sun burns just as bright in mine eyes,
while in yours the tears flow forth and mourn
in the exact same sweet sorrow.
You are just the same as me
and just as the wildflower both blooms and dies,
we too are chained to this jest of fate.
This universal tragedy in beauty's mortality
and so long as we both are seen beneath blue sky
we too, will wither in due time.
Where is it then we should draw the line.

Do we not together in this trial of life
both try to brave the storm,
withstand the flame,
and fight off the demons of ever taunting dark.
So why is it there should be distance between you and me
when we both do revel and bleed.
Torn apart at the seams in the never ending fight,
let us instead mend the fractures of our brutal strife
rather than adding to its plight.
Where both we have marched to the horrid drum
the same battle fought between supposed foes
no, I do not believe it is so.
To ride our chains that shackle all that is dear
we must end the forging hatred that clouds the clear,
the undeniable truth that has always shown so near,
that there is no enemy
for you to be found in here.
In the loving embrace of human tranquility
is all we need for lasting serenity.
But in our callous fear we have lost the way,
it has blinded us all from that which is pure.
Oh what us bitter fools cannot see
that this world isn't just for you or me.
Nature was meant as part of one,
so let us take that divinity
and change what it means to be.
One part in the heart of many,
let us look to the simple wildflower
in order to rediscover.
Hope, in the unity of conviction
that we are not alone
but a piece of greater grandeur
this, our saving rapture.

And just like the wildflower we shall burst into life
spilling through the cracks of uneven ground.
Let us bring to light that which was a lie,
the resounding color that all have muddled
but we.
We both shall be the forbearers to reborn faith,
of generosity and unfathomed grace
this here, shall be our fate.
Not to choke and shove
in order to stay a few minutes in the sun.
But instead our instances of momentary beauty
shall not fade with the passing petal.
And although our roots may not burrow far,
we both shall breath deep into this world
and give life to sullen desert.
let us breed grounds of untouched soil
and let the flowing pastures be humanity.
Left to grow in fields of glory
unmolested by blades or forlorn poison
here, we both shall be the newfound chosen.
Forever changing the mortal act of decaying,
for our imprint is here in the dirt
left fertile for the ages to come.
Paradise without beginning or end.
All there is left to make it so
is to turn back the deceit instilled in time,
and route out all suspicion between you and I.
For beings were never meant for pride,
it is not the truth,
nor is this the way.
Only when it is that we see
that there is no difference between you and me.
Can we defy age old anger

and turn every inch of this hopeful earth,
into a single solitary envision.
So that we can be called once more,
the real and trueborn children
of an actual
Garden of Eden.